A SPELL OF WATCHING

PREVIOUS BOOKS BY HAMISH WHYTE

Poetry
Testimonies (Scotland 1623–1965) (Happen*Stance* Press, 2022)
Paper Cut (Shoestring Press, 2020)
Now the Robin (Happen*Stance* Press, 2018)
Things We Never Knew (Shoestring Press, 2016)
Hannah, Are You Listening? (Happen*Stance* Press, 2013)
The Unswung Axe (Shoestring Press, 2012)
A Bird in the Hand (Shoestring Press, 2008)
Window on the Garden (Essence Press/Botanic Press, 2006)
Christmasses (Vennel Press, 1998)
Siva in Lamlash (minimal missive, 1991)
Rooms (Aquila Press, 1986)
apple on an orange day (Autolycus Press, 1973)

Translations
Envy the Seasons (Tapsalteerie Press, 2022) [with James McGonigal & Iain Maloney]
Martial Mottoes (Galdragon Press, 1998)
Take 5 07 (Shoestring Press, 2007) [contributor]

Prose
Morgan & Me: a memoir (Happen*Stance* Press, 2020)

Edited
Edwin Morgan, *Centenary Selected Poems* (Carcanet Press, 2020)
Ten Poems about Robins (Candlestick Press, 2018)
Scottish Cats: an anthology (Birlinn, 2013)
Kin: Scottish Poems about Family (SPL/Polygon, 2009)
Poems United: A Commonwealth Anthology (SPL/Black & White, 2007) With Diana Hendry
An Arran Anthology (Mercat Press, 1997)
Mungo's Tongues: Glasgow Poems 1630–1990 (Mainstream, 1993)
About Edwin Morgan (EUP, 1990) With Robert Crawford
Noise and Smoky Breath: an illustrated anthology of Glasgow poems 1900–1983 (Third Eye Centre/Glasgow Libraries, 1983)

A SPELL OF WATCHING

New & Selected Poems

HAMISH WHYTE

All rights reserved. No part of this work covered by the copyright herein may be reproduced or used in any means – graphic, electronic, or mechanical, including copying, recording, taping, or information storage and retrieval systems – without written permission of the publisher.

Printed by imprintdigital
Upton Pyne, Exeter
www.digital.imprint.co.uk

Typesetting and cover design by The Book Typesetters
hello@thebooktypesetters.com
07422 598 168
www.thebooktypesetters.com

Published by Shoestring Press
19 Devonshire Avenue, Beeston, Nottingham, NG9 1BS
(0115) 925 1827
www.shoestringpress.co.uk

First published 2024
© Copyright: Hamish Whyte
© Cover photograph: Kenny Whyte

The moral right of the author has been asserted.

ISBN 978-1-915553-53-9.

To my brother Graeme
and in memory of our mother
Alicia Whyte (1923–2023)

CONTENTS

from *apple on an orange day* (Autoloycus Press, 1973)
The Flaw   1
Long Shadows   2
Interview   3

from *Felis Domestica* (privately published, 1975)
The Spell of Watching   4
Locked on the Inside   5

from *Rooms* (Aquila Press, 1986)
Armstrong's Temperance Hotel, Glasgow, 15 April 1908   6
Bay City Blues 26 June 1959   8
Onion   9

from *Siva in Lamlash* (minimal missive, 1991)
Siva in Lamlash   10
Pot Luck   11

from *Christmasses* (Vennel Press, 1998)
Christmasses Now   12
Festive Family Photo   13
Another Christmas Tree Poem   14

from *Sappho Said It* (minimal missive, 2002)
Sappho Said It   15
Your Name   16
Oh   17

from *Window on the Garden* (Essence Press/Botanic Press, 2006)
from Window on the Garden   18

from *A Bird in the Hand* (Shoestring Press, 2008)
A Bird in the Hand   21
Parting at Night: Lleyn   22

Craft	23
Soirée	24
Museum Piece	25
Christina's Commands	26
Guiser	27
First Day in Hospital	28
Postcard from Jura	29
White Wave	30
Between	31
I Miss You When You Sleep	32
Close	33
My Son's Photograph of Shells at Kildonan	34
from Glimpses of My Father	35
Mr Bach (*from* Dreamsters)	36
What the Leopard Said	37
Otis	38
Cornwall to Glasgow	39
Dogsitting in Stockbridge	41
The Great Journey	42
Checkout	43

Uncollected Poems (1967–2011)

Jan	44
Spirit of the Beehive	45
Calendaring	46
Prepositions	48
Last Four Things	49
Three Glasgow Haiku	50
Instead of a Wreath	51
Bidie-In (with Diana Hendry)	52
Hide and Seek with Freya	54

from *The Unswung Axe* (Shoestring Press, 2012)

Winter Coming	55
Horsepower	56
The Unswung Axe	57

Pop-up Babies	58
Bramble	59
Lovemark	60
Where	61
When You're Away	62
See the Ferrets	63
Scones	64
My First Typewriter	65
Drayhorses	66
Finding Chandler	67
All in the Elbow	68
Stockbridge Colonies, Edinburgh	69
Lucky Enough	70
Seagulls in the City	71

from *Hannah, Are You Listening?* (Happen*Stance* Press, 2013)

Child Care	72
Scaffold	73
A Letter to My Long-Lost Uncle	74
The Giraffe in Our Living-Room	75
What the Editor Said	76

from *Things We Never Knew* (Shoestring Press, 2016)

Looking Out	77
Lion	78
Things We Never Knew	79
Grandpa's Boat	80
Dear Fathers	81
Three Taps for Charlie	83
Book Dusters	84
Two Nights in Norfolk	85
StAnza Stanzas	86
I'm Telling You Now	87
The Theatre Royal's Gorgeous Transformation to the Hall of a Thousand Lights	89
Our Jim	90

Sorry	91
La Di Da	92

from *Now the Robin* (Happen*Stance* Press, 2018)

Against Time	93
Signs	94
Slug Ode	95
Mr Scuddery's Speaking Hedge	96

from *Paper Cut* (Shoestring Press, 2020)

Blue Guitar	97
Where's Jemima McGregor?	98
The Precious Ten Minutes	99
Out of the Air	100
A Clean Death	101
A Trick	102
The Waifs of Nairn	103
Paper Cut	104
Editing	105
February	106

New Poems

The Gate	107
First Death	108
Western	109
Hands	110
Kiss	111
Unlimited	112
Fire	113
Round	114

Unfinished Business	115
Shifts	116
Buck Moon	117
An Outing	118
Morning Song	119

A Wet Night in Roslin	120
Argument	121
Heron on the Rocks	122
From the Sea-Window	123
The Moment	124
Archy	125
One for Sorrow	126
Notes	127
Acknowledgements	128

THE FLAW

That golden chain
if stretched to breaking,
my love would drift
on an endless sea;
but the love you gave me
would remain a gift,
as if giving and belonging
were the same.

LONG SHADOWS

The courtyard outside the palace of the emperor
In the bright early morning
Come two returning lovers the dawn in their eyes
To smile at the glaring square of dust
And smile again at their intention
Walk slowly across leaving footprints
Faces composed to laugh the more on the other side
They do not know that in two hours
There will be an execution in the courtyard

INTERVIEW

     I'm an old man
I make seven poems a year
happy shuffling around in slippers
sipping expensive cocktails
paid for by earlier affluence
and current collections of jottings and asides
I must do something about those worksheets
scattered over the floor
sell them to a Yankee uni
I'm content with my room
and shopping lists and menus
food is more important than poetry
sometime friends visit with me
I enjoy cooking –
you needn't sympathise
with any self-pity you think you detect
I have an old poem
to tack on every new thought

THE SPELL OF WATCHING

the
starlings land on the roof
they

worry the cat
who

stares out the window
she

opens her mouth

I
am anchored
I

cannot clap my hands

under the spell of watching

LOCKED ON THE INSIDE

I'm at the window again. Day-dreaming.
It's that or reading detectives stories.
Sometimes a vague sense of urgency, a feeling
Of procrastination in the face of crises:
Radio news of bombs and over-population –
I'm not prepared to die (or kill) for anything.

Apathy at the window. Reading,
Watching, I lose myself and all sensation.
The locked room seems to have more relevance,
The murderer often gets a second chance
Or the choice of suicide: criminals
Can be gentlemen. Or could. In between
Pages I sleep; and my cat will jump up, keen
To look for birds and other animals.

ARMSTRONG'S TEMPERANCE HOTEL, GLASGOW, 15 APRIL 1908

Miss Manners
looks into
a japanned box.
Cards stacked neatly
inside. Finger
nails furrow the green
velvet table
cover.

The atmosphere
is one of quiet
debate. The carriage
clock can be heard
throughout.
The ladies decide
they cannot support
the expense
of taking part in
the monster suffrage
procession in
London. But after
a pause Miss Manners
kindly agrees to
go herself.

Tea is served
lamps are lit.
The ladies
sip and smile.
The minutes
have occupied
only minutes,
representation

will after all
take place
at the capital,
everything is
satisfactory.

Miss Manners
turns her head
like a tortoise.
She wants
to go home,
to sit at
the kitchen table
to write her verse
and eat the
simple sustaining
food she has
prepared beforehand
('that it may be
partaken of
with impunity
at any hour').

BAY CITY BLUES 26 JUNE 1959

In the parking lot
the automobiles
change every week
sometimes every day.
It's hot.
The writer
sits and sweats
in his motel room. He
looks out the window.
When he types
his fingers slip
on the keys.
He can smell
his body odour
and the fish
he fed a stray cat.
He sips at gimlets.
He's trying to write
a novel out of
a gutter world
of graft and blackjacks
molls and gunsters
fall-guys and baby dolls
the edge of the knife
the crack of the wise
put down
with the precision
of Latin
each word
sharp in its place
for two thousand years.
One day
he will own
an Oldsmobile.

ONION
    (for Doris Walker)

every afternoon at four o'clock
I fall asleep
    the room is too busy
the books break their postmeridian silence
      the leaves whisper to themselves
          my papers are restless
             the poems lift
their heads from the page   look
round   sniff the air
    the chair shifts in its carpet grooves
a mist swirls at the top of the bookcase
the ceiling rains
    the lamp switch thunders
        the bulb lightens
           it's all too much
I curl up
  in the mean time
I dig in   wait for the room
to spare me a minute
      another layer grown

SIVA IN LAMLASH

Pine cones burn
tongues of fire
charred voices in the flame:
eighty four thousand mouths
ash for one head.

Smirr drifts across the bay like smoke.

There's a rainbow
at the foot
of Bungalow
Road.

POT LUCK

After afternoon tea at Pirates Cove
Mrs Walker read my leaves. She saw
a new moon lying on its side,
a two-handled cup won by chance,
a broken hunch-back road.

The moon could well have had the old one in its lap,
the cup could have been the loving kind
the shattered road the path of life.
Who knows? Every answer
is an answer.
When in doubt, doubt.

CHRISTMASSES NOW

Christmasses now seem damp and mild
not crisp and apple-cold like then
like our first together: those walks round
Waterfoot, sheepskin mitts, pat the
horse, black and white snaps; picnic to
Portpatrick (French bread, Danish
salami); canoodling in the A
Forty, windows steamed up and all;
families so close we ate two
Christmas dinners, played double games;
exchanged volumes – Soutine
for you, Seferis for me –
being of an age to give each
other art as well as pleasure.

FESTIVE FAMILY PHOTO

Father sprouting Christmas tree
                from his bald patch

Son surprised between pulled faces
                saying cheese

Daughter between sugar and spice
                showing teeth

Mother escaping the picture
                by taking it

ANOTHER CHRISTMAS TREE POEM

At the garden centre
we picked a tree so thick and heavy
it collapsed the first netting machine
and needed a lot of heave to go through
the second. In twenty seven years
we've had all kinds
from desktop decoration to bay window filler
but never one so bushy, green and black –
a forest in itself –
it probably knows what really happened
to Hansel and Gretel.
The cat won't leave the tree alone,
sits behind it, ungetatable,
staring through the lights, the tinsel,
baubles, glass angels, Santa in his aeroplane.
Does he sense a common under-wild,
a resistance to nature as ornament?

SAPPHO SAID IT

many moons ago:
the tongue-tied, the fire
under the skin, blankness
of the eyes, roaring in the ears,
the sweating, the trembling –
the whole enchilada:
untranslatable now
untranslatable then.

YOUR NAME

I can hear my friends saying your name,
the friends I really love, saying your name:
they are saying your name in the tone of voice
I love them for and they are saying your name
with love.

OH

The slight hearing loss
we each suffer from
means we sometimes
fail to catch the sense
of ends of sentences
but what we don't fail
to grasp and gasp at are
the dizzy silent moments
of all this passion stuff –
like the fat magpie
balancing on the phone
wire outside the window:
of course it's going to fall
and of course it doesn't.

from *WINDOW ON THE GARDEN*
(to Diana)

I watch the robin
whirring at the half
coconut shell hang-
ing from the clothes pole –
like a humming bird
it beaks beaks into
the sweet fat and seeds
for its sustenance
and I think of you
hotpenning at your
desk day after day
and the thing I love
is the persistence

*

are we singing
   in the rain?
we are not singing

in the rain
but we like
   the rhinestones
      on the lady's mantle

*

can subconscious topiary
   be making the hedge
      an elephant?

*

picture book of noises:

whirr – lawnmower cutting grass
broom – car starting
squeak – rusty gate
chink – scaffolding going up
buzz – bee on last yellow rose
snore – poet under straw hat

*

Dylan walks on briars
he looks at the dust
he doesn't know his own desires
but he knows who to trust

you've been stung by a wasp
your finger's red and sore
there's no rhyme for wasp
except the word you swore

   Epicurus taught in a garden –
   he said pain was unsatisfied desire –
   you wish
   you'd killed the wasp

*

you turn the earth over
you spruce the garden up
you prune the berberis
you bag the twigs and leaves

the robin hops about
   waiting for you to go

*

now he's at the hanging ball again
flickering in the sun from ball to
berberis and back to ball again

blackbird chasing dunnocks in and
out of the snowdrops – movement and light

*

A BIRD IN THE HAND

In his studio, Matisse,
an old sultan in specs,
sits among cages,
a white dove clasped in his left hand
sketchbook propped on his knee.

Three other doves out of their cage
pose unnoticed by the artist,
looking this way and that
they're extras, a nice ornament top right.

The charcoal gives the single dove
its new shape
its freedom on cartridge:

which might we envy – the bird
fixed for ever on the page
or the dying man
who feels its heart pulsing
through warm white feathers?

PARTING AT NIGHT: LLEYN

I stumbled in the dark down the stony
lane, guided by a flickering
bicycle lamp. I glanced back

to Crowrach Cottage for a light at the window,
saw nothing, turned down the coast road.

She told me later she had watched
from behind curtains, looked for the torch

between hedges, had seen nothing, only
heard church bells in a drowned village.

CRAFT

When we got engaged her father
made me a miniature wooden ladder
(perfectly proportioned
and adjustable to twice its length) –
a hint, I think, at elopement –
saving him the embarrassment
of morning coat, speech, ceremony
and possibly money.

SOIRÉE

You won't sing; you can, but you won't. I cross
the room and jerk the curtains closed: heavy
green velvet shutting out the autumn trees
in the square. I ask again, again you
say no, you don't feel like singing tonight.

You could say it's a question of choice – words
or music, we're the chosen, they take us
or not, they're impervious to special
pleading, best portions or spilt wine (or blood).

But you don't. So I swallow these notions
and go through to the kitchen for coffee.
Above the bubbling percolator I
listen for the sounds of *An die Musik*.

MUSEUM PIECE

To the Art Galleries on a snow-threatened
Sunday afternoon; pushing into
the revolving doors, Kenny and I: wee grey
duffel figure, bulky green coat shuffling behind.
I know he wants to see the dinosaurs,
the foxes (especially the one crunching a bird),
'the armours', even the pictures (to
recognise Degas's *Duranty* I have a postcard of –
'you've got that one' – wish I had) –
but what I think he'd really like, is to go round and
round in the turning doors for ever
and ever, birled without end.

CHRISTINA'S COMMANDS

'Sing golden lumbers'
and we do
and we dance
and we do the hokey-cokey
and turn ourselves about
and play the farmer wants a
and push at swings
and roundabouts
and draw
and read aloud
and 'do it again' till we can't
and stagger off to
'have a nice later'

GUISER

Running the children home
from hallowe'en parties
we passed a fox at the
Crossmyloof Station lights
waiting for the green man.

FIRST DAY IN HOSPITAL
(for Jim Black)

the admission
the wait the pajamas
the leaving behind
the questionnaire
the history and topography of everything I've had
the student nurse Allan ('I'm very interested
                in bowel movements')
the lunch the fly in my soup
the black affronted
the card from Eddie ('hope it does the trick')
the other patients
the cyclist in for vein stripping
the visit by John newly revved and immaculate
                from the clerical outfitters
the first needle the blood sample the odd acceptance of it all
the doctors' round the poke the prod
the do you mind if the lady doctor feels your
the sideways coughing
the tea the bones in the fish
the close shave round my no longer private parts
the too brief visiting time
the cheery anaesthetist ('it used to be horrible')
the news I've drawn first place in the morning
the rush to finish the whodunnit
the lights out
the waiting for thirsty sleep
the screams from another ward
the man in the next bed getting up to go home all night
                patiently led back each time
the thirst
the no sleep
the comforting green plastic wrist tag

POSTCARD FROM JURA

Made soup today –
fried onions in oil
added lentils and stirred
them round a bit
let them sweat
sliced carrots with
your Japanese cut-throat
added those
then water, seasoning, herbs
and the veggie stock cube
you gave me last thing –
all brought to the boil
and simmered –
your recipe but lacking
the essential ingredient.

WHITE WAVE

you are scattered on the water
where rocks burn in the sun
where seals come to sing
where gannets fold and plunge
where sea-thrift keeps its hold
    in all weathers

you are the white wave
blown by the wind
you are the wind
that blows the white wave

BETWEEN

I lie awake
listening to the wind.
There are metaphors
and metaphors but none
to give a roof to this longing
for my new love.
The house creaks slightly.
There is no ghost here
only the absence
of my old love.

I MISS YOU WHEN YOU SLEEP

I miss you when you sleep.
I can see you, swaddled in duvet,
face pressed to the twisted pillow;
I can hear you, breathing steadily,
with occasional low hums –
but you're elsewhere, out of reach –
R and R on some sunny Isle of Words –
dreaming of hunky sonnets, the perfect poem.
If I touched your hair, would desire transmit?
'I'll seduce you in the morning,'
you'd whispered before drifting off.

CLOSE

chopping an onion
the Sabatier slips
stabs my pinky
so quick there's no pain
but blood floods and drips

standing at the sink
cleaning the wound
suddenly want you
close for comfort but
lover not mother
you close close as knife
slide into skin close
as blood seep and not
wash away close
as red
finger-
print

MY SON'S PHOTOGRAPH OF SHELLS AT KILDONAN

washed by the sea
into this abstract rickle
of blues and whites
    mussels cockles whelks scallops
    the odd orange pebble

what draws your eye
is the scrunch of sand
caught in the boat
    of a mussel

it reminds you of the grains –
    found long after the holidays
        gritting the pages of a book
        getting under your nails
            in a trouser pocket

that remind you
    with that slight stound
        of the heart

that remind you

from GLIMPSES OF MY FATHER
    (for my mother)

He fought small but important battles:
he was against the church elders
slow-marching down the aisle
in funereal morning suits
after the offering:
it was the suits particularly –
what was wrong with a simple lounge suit?
(not of course to lounge in) –
he won and the Sunday morning
penguins became men.

*

He once played the piano
for Sir Harry Lauder
at a charity do –
more worried about the great man
(then in his seventies)
falling off the stage
than accompanying him
to the end of the road.

*

Just off the runway
I heard him say to Mum
something about papers in the bureau.
There were six of us on the pleasure flight
from Prestwick in a bi-plane tied
with string, we could see the Heads of Ayr
through the floor –

the only time he and I flew together
but one new thing for father and son to share:
extra-terrestrial fear.

MR BACH (FROM *DREAMSTERS*)
(for Christina)

Mr Bach looked at me from under the bonnet of his green Lincoln convertible. I stopped and looked at him. There was a warm breeze blowing and you could smell the sea. 'Sand,' he said. 'Sand in the magneto.' 'Oh' was all I could offer in reply. I knew nothing about cars. Then he said, 'Listen. Why don't you come in and I'll explain the secrets of my music.' Mr Bach led me into a bright, high-
    ceilinged
room, furnished with only a red grand piano and two wooden
    chairs.
'Sit down, sit down,' he said. We sat on the chairs and he told
    me the
secrets of his music.

WHAT THE LEOPARD SAID

I changed them into diamonds.
I don't remember what they were before.

Maybe they fooled me.
Maybe it was a trick of the light.
Maybe they were always diamonds.

I know I changed them.
I changed them into diamonds.

OTIS

I'd like to see you in my dreams,
old cat: nose pushing at the door
in welcome; warming your snowy
underside at the fire; ginger hovis
on my lap. Instead, I can't help
seeing you in your last minutes
staring at us with blind open eyes,
wheezing as your lungs shut down,
as all of you shut down,
your chin coming to rest
on the table as the drugs took
hold, put you to dreamless sleep.

CORNWALL TO GLASGOW
(*To Edwin Morgan*)

Dear Eddie
How are you
in your yellow room?
I am here in spring
in WSGrahamland
and it's not yellow –
it *is* 'a jasper sea'
and a different water
from the Clyde
(though Graham never
forgot the Clyde) –
it's every shade of green
and pure white breakers
to hurt the eyes
and a blue blue blue
out to America.

What else colours?
as my granny used to say.
St Ives is wearing a coat
of many colours.
In the Tate today
we saw Roger Hilton's
Three Boats
you might have thought
they were autumn leaves
floating on the water.
All the galleries
are stuffed with pictures
of Porthmeor beach
but not one
gets the feeling
of being here

the whole whack
in your face
of sun sand sea rocks –
not even words
can do it either.
I'm sorry you can't
see it for yourself.

I know Graham
invited you once
for a wee holiday
but I don't think
you ever went.

I enclose a postcard
but it's just
what the camera saw.
Next time I visit you
I'll try to show you –
waving my hands
raising my voice –
the splash the light
the u-shaped
pure pleasure
of Porthmeor Beach.

DOGSITTING IN STOCKBRIDGE

stoic (not cynic)
your daughter's dog
Badger hirples along
Glenogle Road –
you can see
where dogged comes from

he lifts his head to stare
at invisible foxes
in the Academy undergrowth
sniffs walls and posts
for the latest news
lavishes more attention
than it deserves
on a scraggy plant
by the Snakey path

bits of him don't work
he has to be wheelbarrowed
up the Dunrobin steps
have his haunches held
over the Bell Place bridge
rewarded with biscuits
after every pee and poo

the cartoon persona
the skewed ambling
the whingeing rug with
the baleful look
the deafness to commands
the interrogation of objects –
he's really an early Greek
philosopher transmogrified
into a woolly liquorice allsort

THE GREAT JOURNEY

The old couple
board the train
make for a table
with facing seats.
The woman says
you sit here
and see where we're going
I'll sit there
and tell you where we've been.

CHECKOUT

We're at the checkout in the Coccimarket,
the main shop in Grez-sur-Loing,
tapping our feet to Johnny Nash –
we're happy for him, he can see clearly now
all obstacles in his way –
he must have been number twenty
of the 20 Greatest Reggae Hits
because he's followed by silence
and the mushrooms never make it
to the scales and the courgettes and onions
don't move and we don't move
and nobody behind us moves –
till Ali snaps a new disc in the machine
and presses play: now we can unpause
pack the mushrooms and the rest
and pay and au'voir
into the bright sunshiny day.

Uncollected Poems (1967–2011)

***

JAN

She walks so fast
you're a sheepdog.

Sings with Wendy
nice to
Wendy her friend.

Different boys
never bothers about
any
always another better.

Her career
has left a trail of broken beds.

She likes dancing on beds.

SPIRIT OF THE BEEHIVE

She stains her lips with blood from a finger
The black cat scratched, a discontented cat
With green eyes. In the mirror her mother's
Lips pout back – guilty, she turns her head
To the door: just her sister stepping on
A loose floorboard or her father scraping
Back his chair in the study through the wall,
Where he sits alone, reading Maeterlinck,
Making notes, Saint Jerome with lion and skull
Behind the desk, lit by the soft yellow
Glow from the honeycomb window.
Her mother, in the kitchen writing to
Her lover, comes alive, like a drowsy bee
Feeding hungrily on orange marmalade.

CALENDARING
   (*for Winifred*)

In from the sun among the cool books:
the desk under the window:
shuffle the folders, untie the tapes.
Seventeen-sixties today, a variety of hands.
Father to son not seen for five years, pen shaky
from affection (or age): his zeal for
improvement: assumption of universal interest
in black cattle and their feed: a story of a cock and bull.
A letter from London. 1768: fire in Pudding Lane
(another one!): papers, ledgers packed to flee: fire put out:
a gulravage at the Blind Harry, enquiries
whether murder were not being committed.

The complete letter each time:
all the news, questions of health, formal intimacies
from loving sons and obedient servants.
Measure the sheets, index
everything and everybody,
main entry under date – an eighteenth century
at a glance, flick through the years,
stick the flicking finger into other people's businesses:
copybooks unopened since blotted,
discharges, sasines, all those precepts
of clare constat, bills of exchange and other exchanges:
progress of land and heir:
the records recorded: different doocots –
hindsight, for the uses of (all for
maybe a line in someone's Acknowledgements?).

Time's up: back out to the dazzle,
train and home. No lamb chop, the healthy nineteen-eighties,
but lentil cutlets. Claret, however, abides.

Bathroom first, scrub off the antique dust.
Particles remain no doubt, go down with the pulse and wine.

We have so little writing – our postcards,
post-its, shopping lists, miss-you scribbles,
plus the greetings of forty years,
will they all go in the bucket when we kick it, never feed
a hungry cataloguer in two hundred years
never get a second reading
glitter again like grains of sand
caught in old ink?

PREPOSITIONS

We walked from Kilchattan Bay
and stopped to picnic
on mutton pies and Blue Ribands
in the ruined inn
at the southern tip of Bute
the place of many a last
Caledonian bite
before the open sea.

LAST FOUR THINGS

She sold the Victorian chaise longue
and most of her jewellery

had the rest of the furniture re-covered
even the piano stool

made sure the three of us knew how
to work the washing machine

lived long enough to hear the Mahler 2
she was too ill to sing in.

THREE GLASGOW HAIKU

Safeway plastic bag
floats past my first-floor window:
where's the messages?

Green domes and frosty
streets: winter sun on Glasgow
glowing like Florence.

Between tenements
the moon hangs huge and golden:
aura of New Year.

INSTEAD OF A WREATH
    (i.m. Barbara Breton Benjamin)

The flowers I'd wanted to send
are not the easiest ones:
the honeysuckle and fuchsia that bound
the hedges of Abersoch, summer of '66,
when we gave each other daft names –
the Wild, the Bold, the Wise, the Sweet –
wrote poems in the sun
sang songs on the beach
drank Chateauneuf-du-Pape, sat
long over coffee and Kit Kat
in the Tarantella, partied
in the greenhouse, trudged
to a soggy sheepdog show
swam at midnight in Henderson's Cove
played 'I Cover the Waterfront'
and covered the waterfront
and, of course, found love.
We've never been back.
Did we ever leave?
We heard the Beach Boys' 'God Only Knows'
and they were, and are, right.
I'd like to think those flowers still grow
in the summer hedges of Abersoch.

BIDIE-IN

Application (DH)

O let me be your bidie-in
And keep you close within
As dearest kith and kin
I promise I'd be tidy in
Whatever bed or bunk you're in
I'd never ever drink your gin
I'd be your multi-vitamin
I'd wear my sexy tiger-skin
And play my love-sick mandolin
It cannot be a mortal sin
To be in such a dizzy spin
I'd like to get inside your skin
I'd even be your concubine
I hope you know I'm genuine
O let me be your bidie-in.

Appointment (HW)

Of course, you may be my bidie-in,
You didn't need to apply within.
A braw new world's about to begin,
We'll gang thegither through thick and thin,
We'll walk unscathed through burr and whin.
If you're to be my porcupin
I'll just have to bear it and grin.
I'll be your sheik, your djinn,
I'll be yang to your yin.
You'll be my kitten, my mitten, my terrapin.
All night long we'll make love's sweet din
And never mind the wheely bin.
In our romantic cin-
ema there'll be no FIN.
And so I say again – you're in –
You've got the job of bidie-in!

HIDE AND SEEK WITH FREYA

She's three and doesn't quite get it.
She likes the hiding bit
but doesn't want not to be found.
We go in the bedroom and look round:
we don't see her
and say so loudly, make a noise
at the door. The duvet quivers and a voice
from under squeaks, 'I'm *here!*'

***

WINTER COMING
   (after Jules Laforgue, 'L'Hiver qui vient')

Rainfall. Nightfall. The wind.
Christmas. New Year.
The chimney in the drizzle.

We can't sit down any more, all the benches are wet.
– that's it till next year –
the benches are wet, the woods have gone to rust –
hear a trumpet play them out!

It's winter coming the season we know so well.
And tonight the wind's done good work:
oh damage, oh nests, oh modest gardens!
Axes echo in my heart, my sleep.

It's the season, it's the season, rust eats at sledgehammers,
eats at the telegraph wires humming
their kilometric blues along empty roads.

It's a melancholy tune (hear the trumpet) –
it's the season, goodbye to grape harvests.
Here's the rain coming with the patience of an angel.

Winter woollies, galoshes, the chemist, dreams,
curtains pulled back from balconies
(those shores of the suburban roof-sea),
lamps, engravings, tea, petits-fours –
will you be my only loves?

No, no, it's the season and the drab planet.
Let the storm unravel the old slippers time knits herself.
It's the season, it's the season.
Every year, every year
I try to give it a tune.

HORSEPOWER

ho ho the horse
puff the puffer
coal to carry
coal to stoke

ho ho the horse
bacon in the galley
sweet tea in the wheelhouse
smoke in the stack
tackety boots
tarry rope

tow horse
go horse

sound hooves
honest engine

ho ho the horse

THE UNSWUNG AXE

The unswung axe rests on a stump
Beside the kindling laid down
While Christmas runs its course.
These Canadian distant cousins
Of my late father-in-law actually live
On Christmas Road, Robert's Creek,
British Columbia. My father-in-law's
Name was Robert. I don't know much
About them except they have a care
For trees and sheep. They're snug
In their wooden house as winter
Drifts the snow around them.
We keep in touch only at Christmas:
They send news of how the seasons treat them,
The occasional family snap, which makes them
Seem even more strangely. But they're thinking
Of us, they hope me and mine are doing well
And the year to come will be fruitful.
They say god bless. I always post a card
With festive greetings and good wishes
For the new year – I do wish them well,
These folk who write me every year
From the farthest reaches of kin.

POP-UP BABIES

It's like an infants' picture book.
Lonely man meets lonely woman
and that's nice
and not so lonely any more.
Then suddenly lonely woman's daughter
has a baby – a jolly boy
a jolly cuckoo in the nest!
OK. They can cope: new skills:
makes life interesting, etc.
Then lonely woman's son
has a baby – a wide-eyed girl.
Lonely man and lonely woman
are even less lonely
but maybe sometimes they pine
for a little loneliness.
Then – what do you know –
lonely man's son's wife's brother
has a baby!
They keep popping up.
Where will it end?
Will lonely man and lonely woman
have to open a kindergarten?

Breaking news – it's reported
that lonely woman's daughter
is expecting another baby.

Oh no.
Oh yes.

BRAMBLE

the give
  of blackberry
    between finger

and thumb
  escape
    of juice

the bounce
  of black pup
    over garden

fence and
  away
    in the trees

LOVEMARK

place

beside

that pang

you want

to ping

again

WHERE

> *where ask is have, where seek is find*
> *where knock is open wide*
>   Christopher Smart, *Jubilate Agno*

Where, is the thing,
not when or how or why –
place and preposition:
we met in the Elephant House
on George IV Bridge
a bolt fell from the blue
and we took it from there.

WHEN YOU'RE AWAY

On the pillow you bash and turn
for coolness I press my face and burn
for you – one body doesn't fit
where two should be – it
misses you and wishes you were here
heart and soul and flesh not mere
space – I roll away from the hot –
loving you even where you're not.

SEE THE FERRETS

Street photographer's snap:
mum, dad and me aged three
with bucket and spade
holiday family at St Andrews –
memory began here
with big sand and sea
the caves I couldn't reach
and best of all the daily walk
back from the beach at teatime
past the garden where the ferrets were
where I'd always want to stop
for those winking somethings glimpsed
through the hedge, that never quite
finished their shapes:
the movement, the strangeness.

In my sunny garden sixty years on
it's dunnocks and robins
I look for hopping out
from under the privet –
but still hope
those old unfixable slivers of light
flitter at me, strain my eyes
to catch whatever it was
whatever it is.

SCONES

The scene is my granny's kitchen.
Dark wood, fire burning, bottle
of Seven Seas Cod Liver Oil
on the mantelshelf (for grandpa's
daily dose). Granny is baking.
And I am 'helping'.
Granny has made me a chef's hat
from yesterday's *Herald* and given me
a small rolling pin and a ball of dough.
I set to rolling out the dough,
squidging it between my fingers,
savouring the slightly sticky
nature of it, shaking the flour,
cutting rounds with the scone-cutter
and putting them in the oven
along with granny's: all equal.

That warm, bright kitchen
of busy love:
a picture
I'd never want not to keep

and best of all – finished scones
to show grandpa
when he comes home from work

and to eat.

MY FIRST TYPEWRITER

My first encounter with a typewriter
was in my grandfather's office –
hardly that: couple of tables
and chairs – and the typewriter,
a hulking Imperial.

Saturday morning: grandpa
would be doing something, checking
viscosity of oil, counting drums,
while I was left at the typewriter,
my task a letter home.

Index finger pushing the big keys down
with all the force of seven years
I clattered out: 'I am i n the office e.
I saw   uncle j imm y and the c ats
in the store.'

Then as now
that tremor
putting life into print.

DRAYHORSES

*('you are exercising your facility
to burble cheerfully')*

Drayhorses are sacrosanct
I said in a dream to Mr Meikle
my old English teacher,
who looked at me with a just
visible curl of contempt
under his walrus moustache:
known as Wally,
pipesmoking, slightly dandy,
hanky peeking from his sleeve.

We endured his benign
dictatorship and red
sarcasm for a year –
he encouraged writing
but liked it neatly penned
and told me fantasy
should always have
one foot on the ground –
fastidious was the word
but how could he be
with snot up his sleeve?

FINDING CHANDLER

Teenage suburban rebels, Bev and I
wore CND badges
to the Young Liberals garden fête:
tucked away behind the book stall
we discovered the real pleasures
of helping unpack and stack:
rummaging for our own treasures –

from a box under the table
came into my hand *The Lady in the Lake*
1954 reprint green and white Penguin
photo of the author on the back
a vaguely academic type with pipe
clutching a black wide-eyed cat –

was it the mocking-Scott title
or the 'Mystery and Crime' the cover promised?
whatever, my very British diet
of Blackwood, Doyle, Christie and Marsh,
James and Stoker was now spiked and spiced:
city-centred, simile-crammed, smart-witted,
sleazy, cynical, sentimental, stylish,
a new world said *read me*.

ALL IN THE ELBOW

In my dream Jerry Orbach from *Law and Order*
sitting in a New York diner
says, 'Kid, ya gotta tuck your culture in your elbow.'
He's probably right.
Where else in your body is so geographic?
It's the part that gets you in and out of situations
the noun that serves as verb
without grammarian's flinch –
goes where hard decisions are needed –
the seat of polish, of humour –
on the inside is the lovers' spot
sensitive to low lights, a cocktail piano, fingertips.
It's all in the elbow.

STOCKBRIDGE COLONIES, EDINBURGH

There are people cleaning up the river.
There are people saving the baths.
There are people measuring the traffic.
There are people mending the paths.

There are people adding windows.
There are people knocking out tunes.
There are people snipping the overhang.
There are people mooning at moons.

There are people living together.
There are people living apart.
There are people living singly.
There are people marrying their art.

There are people bringing up babies.
There are people keeping parents fed.
There are people walking dogs and poems.
There are people remembering the dead.

LUCKY ENOUGH

A spring day by the Water of Leith:
I happened to turn my head in time
To see a heron catch up an eel
And take off, the eel a black wriggle
In its beak: a decisive moment: a haiku.
First thought, a lucky sighting;
Then somehow a wish to rewind, back
Along the path, to notice the heron
Standing in the river, motionless,
Patient, watching the water –
And leave it there.

SEAGULLS IN THE CITY

Hearing them above
you want the lane to wind to a harbour
not the West End bus stop.

In George Street a baby herring gull,
fluff ruffled by the cold wind,
stands staring through the glass doors
of THE PIER shop –
can it read? can it pun?

In Princes Street Gardens
mother black-backed and son
put on their own Fringe show:
Tough Love on the East Coast
(in Gull, no surtitles).
Feed me cries the son;
the mother ignores him, his beaking –
feed me he cries
with method school squawking.
Feed yourself
we know her silence says.
Their performance wins them chips
thrown bravo by tourists.
Encore is the tragi-comedy
A Short Fight for the Last French Fry.

CHILD CARE

Mention the children's playpark
and you picture it by Brueghel or Bosch:
little bodies ruined by fiendish torture machines,
heads split open, hangings from rigging,
falls from the top of a slide, falls from the side
of a slide, arms broken, legs smashed.
You dread grandson and granddaughter
shouting *Yes! Let's go to the playpark*:

dread dread dread and the what-if blame –
oh the scope for losing them.
Charades? you suggest,
knowing there's no escape from their urge to run,
climb things, stick their noddles through holes.
Love them, love their danger.

SCAFFOLD

Any scaffold's a dangerous
construction.

These four men as they climb
two storeys to the roof
are so practised they hook
us like circus performers.

They're so relaxed they can afford
to be daft: one hangs over
and swings his arm like a monkey;
one leans nonchalantly rolling
a cigarette.

A piece of planking floats upwards
like an Indian club, casually
caught with one hand by the man
at the top, the only one without
a hard hat, the one who slots the poles
in the holes with unfailing
accuracy.

There's a moment of rest; they pose
one above the other as if for
an illustration in a picture book.
They've reached that pinnacle
of art, making the difficult look
easy-peasy.

A LETTER TO MY LONG-LOST UNCLE

Why write now, when you're long gone?
Rummaging in the archive box the other day
I came across a photograph of you
in your ANZAC uniform, about 1915,
a sheepish grin memento.
My mother said you'd been an engineer
building Australia's roads and I imagined you
tenement boy spooling into the outback.

That's what she was told. But now Aunt Myra,
your daughter, says not roads but railroads –
just a slight adjustment of romantic notioning:
you're still my grandpa's brother, great-uncle Sam,
who went off down under.

I have a picture and a story and that's enough
in a world that bleats *family family*,
that asks who do I think I am,
where Google knows nearly everything.

THE GIRAFFE IN OUR LIVING-ROOM

Possibly as strange to passing folk
as the one the Ming admiral brought back
to China in 1406, our giraffe
stands at the window in hat and scarf.
We call her Carmen, we talk to her, and
prefer her to any old elephant
in the room. She's that rare thing,
a listening creature who wisely says nothing.
Cheaper than a therapist,
more meditative than a Buddhist,
she embodies being and is-ness.
She looks out and in, and this
is her strength: maybe seeming odd at first sight,
she is – long neck, happy smile – just right.

WHAT THE EDITOR SAID

good idea well followed through we enjoyed
a great deal we read with pleasure and interest
there was much to take note of the bustle and
jar the excursion and homeward turn some
belters of poems got hold of my ears all well-
crafted precise rhyming we particularly liked
numbers three four and seven but

LOOKING OUT

I'm looking out for the robin,
the robin's looking out for me.
What we have between us is crumbs:
today a mix of poppy bloomer and Rice Krispies.
I say *chook-chook* the way my grandfather did
to call the birds to his garden (if he wasn't out
early enough the blackbird would
tap on the window).

And here he is, swaying on the clothes line,
eyeing me brightly. I shake the crumbs
from the tub and go in. Soon I'm at my desk,
looking out again; robin's still there –
each of us pecking away: he's got his
sustenance, I've got mine.

LION

Walking up from the river
the flood defence man
in his orange helmet
   and yellow high-vis jacket
whistles back to the blackbird
singing out from the cherry blossom.

A cat pads past and the trill
turns to warning.
'That cat,' the man says to his mate,
'is a lion.'

There's a breeze
and petals drift down
   like flakes of snow.

THINGS WE NEVER KNEW

Sometimes when I visit my mother
we go through her old photographs.
I once asked about this handsome chap
in uniform. 'Oh, that's Arthur,' she said.
'He was in the Royal Engineers.
Went off to the war and left his kit box,
but never came back' – solving
the mystery of the chest in the loft
with odd initials stencilled on it.
'He was the one before your father.'

At the door she called after me,
'Don't you dare put that in a poem.'

GRANDPA'S BOAT

Grandpa told the tape recorder
the story of the boat
he bought in Campbeltown harbour
for thirty or forty pounds
with the idea of putting in a tank
to supply fishermen with oil,
but the fishing fell off
and the boat lay for, oh, many a day;
he went to inspect it
and a man came up from the galley
and told him to get off
but grandpa told him he was the owner
and he was going to scrap it –
oh, said the man, he'd been living there
for three months.

So the boat was scrapped
and the Campbeltown farmers got new gates
and good oak posts and grandpa got ten pounds
back – like the steam roller that rolled
down the Rest and Be Thankful,
the empty distillery and its no copper,
the rubber glove mountain –
another dead loss to the firm.

DEAR FATHERS

1.

Dear father
all those years
you composed at the piano
I scribbled upstairs in my room
we never wrote a song together.

2.

Dear father-in-law
whenever I see thyme
I think of your garden
and how you let it grow
over the path: bitter-sweet
scent every footstep.

3.

Dear father of my father
I hardly knew you
but I still use your tools
and your bunnet
hangs in the hall.

4.

Dear father of my mother
I loved your search
for meaning beyond
the good deal
and the way you mended things
with chewing gum.

5.

Dear me

THREE TAPS FOR CHARLIE

My white mouse
had a skin condition
and couldn't stop
scratching his face.

Grandpa put him to sleep
with a plastic bag
and the gas poker.

We buried him
in the garden
under a tree
with a ritual
grandpa invented

that we'd repeat
every time
we passed the grave.

BOOK DUSTERS

There's cliffs
of books
for us dusters
at the National
Library of Scotland.

We're at the
bookface
inch by inch
year by year
we climb we traverse
we keep the dust off
millions.

It's satisfying
it's not boring
every book
is different
the leather the cloth
the fancy the plain
there's time
to scan titles
some pretty
odd ones
I can tell you.

It's like painting
the Forth Bridge
without the fresh air
and fear
of drowning.

TWO NIGHTS IN NORFOLK

and I've seen it all:
the more sky
the flat green the flat rape
the focus on trees
the thatched the crumbling brick
the marriage of mod cons and quaint
the fields of pigs and pig arcs
the ten ducklings on the mere
the wandering cockerels
the 'publishing' bookshop that doesn't publish
the Lowestoft cod (on a Norfolk menu) and the too many chips
the tattoo on a boy's neck ('fight off your demons')

the lack of ghosts haunting the old coaching inn
   in which Charles II once broke his fast
   (I had the full veggie: baked beans, one egg, three
   half tomatoes, three mushrooms, triangle of fried bread) –

     where were the roasted choir boys and the jilted lady in white?

StAnza Stanzas

We were getting up from the table
after our kippers and poached eggs
in the basement dining room
of the Albany Hotel, St Andrews,
during the annual poetry festival,
when the fire alarm went off and we all
had to go outside to windy North Street.

A fire engine arrived and khaki men
clomped into the building – to the delight
of two wee boys and a woman writer
who had herself photographed leaning
against the red machine like a car ad. All
clear – only teenagers with an aerosol.
We crowded back, some to the lounge,
some to their rooms, most funnelling down
to their unfinished breakfasts. The poet
Durcan was standing on the stairs,
bag in hand; he looked at us
milling about. 'Where are you all going?'
he squawked. 'Where are you all going?'

I'M TELLING YOU NOW

Dear Sixties

I remember you
God only knows
it was a strange brew
but a wonderful land –
good vibrations here there and everywhere
love was all around –

no particular place to go:
homeward bound or Route 66
even meet on the ledge
or halfway to Paradise (if it's half as nice).

Why *do* fools fall in love?

There was something in the air,
blowing in the wind.
We heard it through the grapevine
tried not to lose that loving feeling.

Dancing in the streets.
Crazy.

All or nothing: I was a believer,
a dedicated follower.
We had all the time in the world.

Then ha ha said the clown, it's all
over now – 96 tears and a hard day's night.

A summer holiday
in my life, a sunny afternoon.
But if you gotta go, go now.
Hello, goodbye.
Thank you very much.

THE THEATRE ROYAL'S GORGEOUS TRANSFORMATION TO THE HALL OF A THOUSAND LIGHTS

As fast as Glasgow burned its theatres to the ground
it built them back again – we couldn't do
without our plays and tunes, we need a dance
and song to keep us going. This gaff's given us
the lot: couthie comics, rude rhymes, romance,
camp and catchphrase, flicks (with music), Ali Baba's
thieves, diverse monsters (Mary Shelley's, Columba's),
wafting Rhine Maidens, our very own Marie Loftus,
a masked ball, a harlequinade, a circus,
Dan Leno's *Orlando Dando*, Henry Irving,
and Sarah Bernhardt for one matinee only –
not to mention the sensational telly
(*One O'Clock Gang* still daft in the memory).

Whatever walls come down, go up, go round,
this magic box holds all, swirling, birling
in the waiting darkness the works shine through.

OUR JIM

sitting on the sofa together
with our mugs of coffee
waiting for Jim to mend
the washing machine

(he's in the kitchen singing
and puffing with the heat
– 'I'm leaking' he says –
as he replaces
the burned-out brushes)

it's very companionable
not quite like
our evening side by side
watching telly
more like listening
to a short story
on the radio
more aware of each other
and of course
with a common anxiety
and thoughts of the full
laundry basket –

later at supper we'll talk
about all the wee things
that bother us now
and how difficult it is
to remember how we felt
to recreate how we really felt
at particular times and places
long ago

SORRY

I'm sitting in the waiting room
the computer check-in's on the blink
I've been forgotten someone's taken ahead
of me I've no book and I'm not touching
that dog-eared *Country Life* so I sit still
enjoying the ebb and flow of patients
and reading the notices about missed appointments
and giving up smoking then a couple come in
arguing the man effing and blinding
a chap in a pin-striped suit asks him politely
to moderate his language he says he's sorry
he didn't mean to offend he apologises again
and goes on saying he's sorry until you want
the effing and blinding back at that point
the receptionist opens the door and asks me
if I am who I am sorry about the delay
the doctor will see me now.

LA DI DA
   (*for Sarah Keast*)

rowing boat
keep afloat

state I'm in
sink or swim

choppy sea
look at me

feather oar
pull for shore

ship your oar
ask for more

harbour light
home tonight

AGAINST TIME

The blue tits flit
at the coconut shell hanging
from the clothes pole,
empty it of fat
dab by dab.

They're anxious birds,
always on the *qui vive*,
they don't seem to know
the other birds
prefer ground fodder.

I sit at the window
and watch them
going about their survival.
I'm anxious too, about many things –
though not about lunch.

SIGNS

this morning in January
the garden holds not much
in the way of earthy delight
branches bare
brown leaves drifted here
and there the green
without shine

but a few snowdrops
show their white tips
robin flashes his breast
balancing for a sec
on the berberis
the nut-holder on the clothes
pole swings at the pecking
of a great tit

it's my father's birthday
and though he died over
thirty years ago that space
of blank memory can still
be dotted with signs of his life
the family photos plus tapes
of him playing the piano
and the occasional startling
sound of his voice

SLUG ODE

O slug
slugging across
the damp grass
negotiating
soggy leaves

so slow

do you know
where you're going?
or like RLS
just believe
in going?

MR SCUDDERY'S SPEAKING HEDGE

Today the hedge is talking in whispers.
With a slight breeze and birds singing
it's hard to hear.

Don't listen to me, I'm just shudder
and rustle, comb and paper
to the wind. You need

the birds, their sounds you translate
into approximates. Mr Scuddery
didn't plant any answers with me.

So sit there in the showers of blossom
swirling from the cherry, listen to the birds,
think up a haiku, but don't write it down.

BLUE GUITAR

At the tea dance in the village hall
this sunny Saturday afternoon
Derek is trying out his new guitar
his blue guitar
his Fender Stratocaster –
he's been strumming along
as Roy sings 'Moon River'
but now it's time for his solo:
he plays the tune almost straight,
with just the right amount
of twang to make it sound
like it never has before
(a new species of wistful)
and give the douce waltzers
goosebumps.

WHERE'S JEMIMA MCGREGOR?

'Jemima McGregor?' the nurse called
in the osteoporosis waiting room.
Everyone looked round.
'Jemima McGregor?' she called again.
'Oh well. Mr Blainey then.'
An old man in pink shirt and shorts
got up and shuffled after her.

We wondered what had happened
to Jemima McGregor.
We knew the risks, the bone density stats,
the constant fear of fracture.
Had she fallen? Had she broken
her hip, her pelvis, her ankle?

Jemima McGregor was called twice more
but never appeared.
We thought about her for days.

THE PRECIOUS TEN MINUTES
(for Ian Davey)

The GP stands at the door of his room,
shakes my hand, asks me how I am.
I always smile and say fine, except for …
this niggling problem
or I'm here for a checkup
or a repeat prescription
or something.

He listens.
He's a cautious man, gets me tested
in case: 'Let's be sure.'

He sounds me out about an ongoing condition:
if I can live with it
he can live with it.
'As long as you can do the things
you want to do.'
He knows I'm a worrier.

I don't feel rushed.
It's a conversation.
It all seems as it should be.

OUT OF THE AIR

Here's a photograph
of my father's father Thomas
of the fledgling RAF Photographic Unit
having a break and a look at the paper.

Then it'd be back to high-speed
developing and printing the special
thin negatives, eighty enlargements
an hour rushed to Intelligence:
aerial snaps of the German fleet
destroyer after destroyer.

Or aboard a drifter in the North Sea
fishing pilots out of soggy wrecks,
camera always at the ready; catching
the progress of a torpedo in amazing
freeze-frame or folk on a Hush ship
launching a plane.

All in a day's work. Turn another
page of the album he put together
after the war and it's more
leisure pics: pals at the mess table,
resting on a hill, the tell-tale sign
of the local pub: grabbed moments
during the final push:

six million prints
in the ten months
before Armistice.

A CLEAN DEATH

Mother's father
Robert Berry
railway clerk
at Buchanan
Street Station
read the papers:
columns
of the slaughtered
in the trenches –
enough to decide
to enlist
in the Navy:
if he died
it would be at sea.

A TRICK

The princess stared at the man
as he put his hand into his trouser
pocket and brought out a white
horse. He mounted the horse
and rode away, calling over
his shoulder, 'Don't follow.'

But she did and trudged for months
through dense forests and dark valleys
asking people on the way if they had seen
a magician on a white horse.

She eventually arrived at a village
half-way up a mountain where she'd heard
he lived. She found him at a water trough
in the sunlit square letting his horse drink.

He looked at the princess and smiled
and put the horse back in his pocket.
They were married and lived happily
in a gingerbread house for fifty-one
years with his mother.

THE WAIFS OF NAIRN
    (for Kate Ashton)

The waifs of Nairn are numerous.
Each one is a skelf of a girl.
They're blonde and they all wear black
and work in hospitality.
They are kind and charge you only £2
for two filter coffees and shortbread as
the steamer's broken. One is pregnant and
can't eat haggis and tells us how she wants
to give her son a better start in life than she had
and makes us cry, at no extra charge.
The hotel waif says they don't have postcards,
try the newsagent's, which I do but they're
closed, though through the window I can see
another waif, standing by herself at the counter.

PAPER CUT

Four hundred years ago
you could have
your ears cropped
for publishing
seditious pamphlets.

Tonight, taking
my latest slim vol.
from my rucksack –
innocuous poems
about birds and gardens –
I nicked my finger
on the cover,
drew blood.

How strangely pleasing
the printed page
can still do damage.

EDITING

sitting by the fire
each on our couch
my eyes are closing
over the *TLS*
I'm drifting off
but can still hear
your pages turn
your pencil write
you're reading poems
making notes
I pick these sounds
as you pick out
the poems you like
and this must be
one of the most
companionable
forms our love takes
so ordinary
we don't remember
but won't forget

FEBRUARY

time
for snow and snowdrops
reminder
of that chancy
visitor love

New Poems

***

THE GATE

'I saw you,' said the snooty woman
from round the corner. 'I saw you
swinging on my gate. You
were wearing
a yellow
jumper.'

I did indeed
have a yellow
jersey, knitted
by my granny.
But it wasn't
me on the gate.
It wasn't me
seventy
years
ago.

FIRST DEATH

was Granny Whyte, Dad's mother.
I was very young, I took it comfortably
enough, sitting on the kitchen stool
staring through the open door –
we had blackcurrants and raspberries then
in the back garden. She was part
of my summer holidays for a while,
taught us card games in the sun lounge
when it rained, like strip jack naked,
and I beat her at draughts, unaware
of the child's privilege of allowing
his elders to win. When we came home
from Arran there were rasps to be picked
if birds and neighbours hadn't got them
first. I'd gone with my father to see her
in hospital: a damp night, we changed
trams, I sat at the foot of the bed
reading space comics while they talked.

WESTERN

One day after school
Billy Anderson and I
were Red Indians.
We captured Christine Keir
and tied her to a lamp post
in Kilpatrick Gardens
and whooped round her
as per the braves
in our comics.
An old woman saw us
and banged on the window.
We unloosed our prisoner
who didn't seem to mind.
Nowadays, we'd say
it was consensual.

HANDS

Ishbel and I were chucking
a tennis ball about the clubhouse:
I missed a catch and the ball
whacked the back of my hand.
She immediately grabbed my wrist
and dragged me into the toilet
and ran cold water over it.
I was startled at the speed
and the expertise, but enjoyed
the early teenage surrender
to another's care.

KISS

Jane and I were standing
on a bridge looking
at the water below.
She turned, took my head
in her hands and kissed me
full on the lips. Too amazed
to resist I went with it, put
my arms round her and forgot
the crowds of beachgoers
milling about.

We were nineteen, students
on summer vacation hotel work.
We'd gone for an afternoon walk,
as friends I thought. I thought
she fancied Pete the barman.
I knew nothing.

She held my hand on the way back.
I remember the scent of honeysuckle
from the hedges along the road.

UNLIMITED

At the age of seventy Grandpa sold
the Scottish Lubricating Oil Company
Limited and retired to Troon
to grow potatoes and onions
and play golf.
He bought a house close
to Fullarton course –
a few yards down the road,
he just had to hop over the wall.
He found a neighbour, an old minister,
to partner (and philosophise with).
In the back garden he made sure
Granny had her roses
seen from the kitchen window.
He laid out the washing green
for family putting as well.
Oh the happy holes in one
and howking the balls
from the shaws!

FIRE

A Thursday night, September 1967, I'm
watching *Top of the Pops* with Grandpa.
He's seventy-seven and loves *Top of the Pops*.
His favourite group is The Seekers and
'wee Pearly Gates', as he calls Judith Durham.
He loves, he says, to see the young folk
shaking themselves out of the old ideas.

On our black and white screen appears
a gyrating man with clearly flames
shooting out of his head. It's
The Crazy World of Arthur Brown.
Not Moonshine Honeyspinner or
Taggle the Gypsy or Ludwig Pumpernickel
but ordinary Arthur Brown
with flames shooting out of his head
and he's screaming 'Fire!' all the time
like he's the devil. 'I'll take you to burn!'

Is he saying we've had the summer of love
now it's payback for hippiedom and
flowers in your hair and all that dippy stuff?
Who knows? Arthur's certainly disturbing
and I've no idea what Grandpa makes of him.
It's a far cry from the waltzes of his youth.
Maybe he's thinking of the pearly gates.

ROUND

It's 1977, March.
I'm up early, 5a.m.
to be collected
by Sheila in her
yellow Renault 4
who is running me
to Loughborough
to see my friend Neil.
Winifred's up as well
though pregnant with
the future Kenny.
Quick cup of tea
in the kitchen.
I happen to look
between curtains
at the back of
the tenements
opposite.
Through a half-
open window
I see a lighted
room and naked
bodies dancing
in a circle.
Is this the Queen's
Park coven
celebrating spring
equinox with
a witches round?

UNFINISHED BUSINESS

Me, I'm mainly on the edge of things
but I see what goes on.
We're a pretty tight-knit crew really,
going round the country
putting on these 'rallies' you might call them.
There's the boss of course, top bloke,
people love him, gift of the gab,
exudes hope, says we needn't be
under-the-thumbs.
The main man's Pete, a tough cookie,
then his china Andy – he organizes
the purvey, got an in
with a baker's and a fishshop.
And we all love Tommy, he's a pal,
though we're not quite sure –
bit of a question mark. I'll just
mention Jim – nimble
as a bee in a tar barrel – but loyal, oh yes.
The rest of us are backup.
However. There's a hitch. There's a snitch.
There's always a snitch.
He *would* be the guy looks after the dough.
Too fond of the shekels that one.
Anyway. Long story short, he dobbed in the boss.
And that was that.

SHIFTS

He watched the two girls –
sisters –
he thought them beautiful
in their cream shifts,
their hair dark, curly,
slightly wild –
each holding a little
suitcase.

Their father stood quietly,
the mother fussed,
then put the girls on
the train.

He waited till
they waved
before arresting
the parents.

BUCK MOON

Big moon
brighter than ever
rising over
the rooftops.

Oh, Anne of Green Gables,
call it down,
bounce it along,
bowl it like a hoop!

Show us
what we can do
with a dab
of imagination.

AN OUTING

They trekked across Fenwick Moor
They climbed Ballageich
They ate their picnic there and drank piña coladas
    from a cool box
They admired the wind turbines whirling away
    a whole family of them
They kept their cagoules on because of the gale
    which almost blew their beanies off
They said 'exhilarating' more than once
They were happy until it rained
They didn't have waterproof trousers
They phoned an uber to take them home

MORNING SONG

It's 5.30am. I open the door
to put out the charity bag on the stoop
for collection (must be before 7)
and I'm hit by an avian wall of sound:
the Lothian Blackbirds Community Choir
(no other bird gets a cheep in)
the loudest trilling I've ever heard
it's thrilling – unhummable
but thrilling.

A WET NIGHT IN ROSLIN

A wet night in Roslin
The Self Righteous Brothers
are playing a charity do
at the British Legion Hall.
They've arrived early
to set up and sound check.
Harmonica Dave organizes
a lot of wattage, singer Dave
goes out in the rain to find Dino's
and bring back fish and chips
for guitar Chris, pizza for drummer
Hamish and burger for double bass
Daniel, nothing for himself, not
before a gig. Singer Gail comes
later, has a large glass of water.

Audience assembling, noisy, drinking,
eyeing up the raffle prizes, a good
turnout for a wet Friday night.
It's half past eight. It's time.
The band kicks off with a funky 4/4
'Cissy Strut', singer Dave reappears
from beyond the double rainbow,
cuts the music, says a few words intro,
finger-snaps 'Mack the Knife' into
life and away we go.

ARGUMENT

In *Wilde Lake* by Laura Lippman
I read the sentence
'AJ had grown dangerously fond of arguing.'
and I remembered
my own teenage growing fondness for arguing:
mainly at the tea table
mainly with my mother
mainly about meanings.
The back and forth made my brother cringe
and get off as fast as he could
while I ground on
intent on getting it right
on being right.

HERON ON THE ROCKS

For some reason this heron
is not going to budge from
this bit of rock.
The seagulls are confident
it's theirs. They dive-
bomb the heron who stabs
his beak at them and squawks.
One gull tries solo without luck
then rounds up its mates
and they all have a go.
After ten minutes of near-hits
the heron says, 'Sod this
for a game of sailors'
and flaps off. A gull follows
to make sure he beats it.
They all cry victory
and settle down before
the tide comes in.

FROM THE SEA-WINDOW

The morning tide's going out.
The heron stalks the rock pools.
A dunlin picks its way through the seaweed.
A black poodle paddles in the shallows.
The ladies who swim wade ashore
    and take off their wetsuits and pink floats.
The heron has solidified
    and waits.
On the flat rock a baby gull runs
    to catch up with its mother.
On another rock some shags form a line.
Offshore a lobster boat checks the creels.
Glint of sun on water – it's taken till now
    till nearly twelve for things to move
    and me to nod off over Penelope Shuttle's poems,
dreaming of salt and clothes pegs.

THE MOMENT

two lovers stop
    at the sea wall
arrange their faces
    for a selfie
she loosens her hair
    from its band
he finishes chomping
    an ice cream cone

portrait or landscape
    they can't decide
they try both ways
    heads close together
as they can

his arm round her
    they smile
into their past
    present and future

ARCHY

I write emails (and some poems)
in lower case because
my hero is Don Marquis's
Archy, the cockroach
possessed by a poet's soul
who wrote his poetry
on an old typewriter
without using caps
not because he thought
he was E.E. Cummings
but because he couldn't work
the shift key
being only an insect
and not strong enough
but he was a poet
his first words were
'expression is the need of my soul'.

ONE FOR SORROW

Walking up the road from the station
for the last time to my mother's flat
for the final day of clearance
I noticed a solitary magpie in a tree
hopping from branch to branch,
no sign of its mate.

In the lobby I met two blokes
humphing a large wooden box
down the stairs. 'That's mum's
sewing machine,' I said. 'Aye,'
said one of the men. A huge part
of her life: early married days
she made her own clothes –
I remember the tissue patterns
laid out on the floor.

At the back of the hall cupboard
my brother and I found a gold tray
which we knew instantly
as the one we had our meals from
when we were ill in bed.
We threw it out.

NOTES

'Armstrong's Temperance Hotel' – Miss Manners was a real person, to be found in the pages of the Minutes of the Glasgow Women's Suffrage Society, held in the Mitchell Library, Glasgow. The quotation is from *The Women's Suffrage Cookery Book*, compiled by Mrs Aubrey Dowson (Women's Printing Society, n.d.).

'Bay City Blues' – the date is the date of Raymond Chandler's death.

'A Bird in the Hand' – based on the photograph by Henri Cartier-Bresson.

'Cornwall to Glasgow' – W. S. Graham: William Sydney Graham (1918–1986), poet, born Greenock, lived mostly in Cornwall; old friend of Edwin Morgan's.

'Spirit of the Beehive' – title of Spanish film by Victor Erice, 1973.

'Calendaring' – archival term for cataloguing papers chronologically; here, the Bogle Family Papers in the Mitchell Library.

'Bidie-In' – Scots term for live-in lover.

'La Di Da' – print by the artist Sarah Keast which has these lines running along the oars of a boat. The so-called 'la di da' foot is a cretic, a three syllable metrical foot with one unstressed syllable between two stressed ones, e.g. 'fish and chips'.

ACKNOWLEDGEMENTS

I'd like to thank all the editors and publishers who took a chance on publishing my poems over the years, especially John Bishop, David Neilson, Carl MacDougall, Jim Green, Duncan Glen, Richard Price, Gael Turnbull, Gerry Cambridge, Joy Hendry, Gerry Loose, Julie Johnstone, Helena Nelson and, not least, John Lucas of Shoestring Press.

Most of the poems in the 'Uncollected' section appeared in the following: *GUM* [*Glasgow University Magazine*], *Glasgow Herald*, *Herald*, *The Frogmore Papers*, *Chapman*, *The Coffee House*, *Handfast* (SPL/Polygon). The two heron poems in the New Poems section appeared in *Wild Court*. Thanks to the editors.

I'm immensely grateful to so many for friendship and/or encouragement (not to mention sharp critical eyes) in poetical matters, especially Irving Benjamin, Linda Benzie, Simon Berry, Tom Berry, Donald Beveridge, Rosemary Bower, Gerry Cambridge, Stewart Conn, Elizabeth Cook, Derek Copland, Alan and Helen Durndell, Anne Escott, Joe Fisher, Sheila Forrest, Janice Galloway, Frank Glynn, Anne Harrison, Kate Hendry, Kevin McCarra, James McGonigal, Catherine McInerney, Neil McLellan, Robyn Marsack, Edwin Morgan, Joe Murray, David Neilson, Helena Nelson, Donny O'Rourke, Richard Price, Mike Redwood, Alasdair Robertson, John Swinton, Gael Turnbull, Leslie Verth, Carmela Vezza, Brian Whittingham, Brent Young, Pat and John Young.

And I'd like to pay tribute to my poetry workshop chums, Christine De Luca, Ian McDonough and Diana Hendry, for continuing nourishment.

Thanks too to my family, especially my late wife Winifred, son Kenny and daughter Christina, for love and support.

Kate Hendry, Stewart Conn and Elizabeth Cook cast their eyes over these poems and made valuable suggestions – many thanks.

Diana Hendry, partner in life and poetry, deserves most credit for this book, with huge thanks and love for love and propulsion: *mentiens iter*, as Catullus says